And So I Was Blessed

Also by Bunkong Tuon

Gruel (NYQ Books, 2015)

And So I Was Blessed

Bunkong Tuon

To Deb Harman —

Here's a story of my father's
family in the Mekong Delta
in southern Vietnam.

I am grateful
for your friendship!

[signature]

Union College

9-17-2018

NYQ Books™

The New York Quarterly Foundation, Inc.
New York, New York

NYQ Books™ is an imprint of The New York Quarterly Foundation, Inc.

The New York Quarterly Foundation, Inc.
P. O. Box 2015
Old Chelsea Station
New York, NY 10113

www.nyq.org

First Edition

Set in Times New Roman

Layout by Raymond P. Hammond

Cover Design by Raymond P. Hammond

Cover Art: Taken by the author on a trip to see family in the Mekong Delta

Author Photo by Nicole M. Calandra

Library of Congress Control Number: 2017948480

ISBN: 978-1-63045-052-6

And So I Was Blessed

ACKNOWLEDGMENTS

No poet is an island. I am grateful, then, to the country of my birth, Cambodia, my home country, the United States, and the beautiful country, Việt Nam; to the friends who combed through the many versions of this book and offered invaluable comments: Jim McCord, David Kaczynski, Floyd Cheung, Tony Gloeggler, Clint Margrave, Harry Marten, Jordan Smith, Kara Doyle, Alan Catlin, Ted Jonathan; to April Selley for her eternal friendship; to colleagues in the English Department at Union; to Lana Cao, Mark Jones, and my students from Union College and William Hobart Smith College; to Raymond Hammond for his generous support and guidance; and last but certainly not the least, to my wife and daughter.

Earlier poems previously appeared in *Poetry Quarterly*, *Consequence*, *Mekong Review*, *Misfit Magazine*, *Silver Birch Press,* and *Gruel* (NYQ Books).

"To the Blue-Eyed and Blonde-Haired Girl in a Hmong Village in Northern Việt Nam" borrows words for embroidery symbols from HmongEmbroidery.Org

CONTENTS

Preface

Part I

Part II

Part III

Postscript

for Stella

Preface

Waiting for Your Arrival

Last night a green dragon
rose from the ocean's blue water.
Wings spread wide to keep
us cool against the sun's rays.

A quiet joy flutters in
our chests as we wait.

Part I

Friend

My friend asked,
"Why Vietnam?
They're our enemy.

The Khmer Rouge were
trained by the Vietnamese.
Look at what they did to us!
They may have Khmer bodies,
but their minds are Vietnamese!"

Shaking head, heaving chest,
"Untrustworthy rats!
They dig tunnels and eat dogs.
You watch what you eat there."

I said, "Thanks, buddy."

His brows furrowed.
"Just looking out for you, brother."

Enemy

The woman sat
in the window seat.
I had the aisle seat.
"Vietnamese?"
She asked as we flew
over the South China Sea.
The space between us
felt louder than
the plane's engine.
I said, "To Hà Nội. You?"
"Saigon," she nodded.

She then mentioned
a district that sounded familiar,
a village where my father's mother
still lives, where my father was born,
my father who left his home.
With thick curly gray hair
the woman looked like my aunt.

The flight attendant brought her cart
of neatly packaged food.
My neighbor looked at the options
and pointed to the chicken with rice.
I chose beef, also with rice.
We ate quietly.
Then the woman touched
my shoulder and held out a bowl
of chicken salad.

After dinner my neighbor
covered her mouth
as she picked her teeth

with a toothpick.
She then reached into her purse,
handed me a stick of gum,
and smiled.

Late Arrival in Hà Nội

At the taxi counter,
I gave my hotel's address,
and waited.
The night air was cool.
The airport empty
of travelers.
A driver walked in
and took my luggage.
I followed behind.
In the backseat
I sat in the middle
studying the taxi driver,
looking out the window
to make sure I wasn't
driven into some alley.
I prayed with dry lips,
thought about my parents,
and asked for their help.
The driver was young,
slender, smaller than me.
If things got sketchy
I could take him.
He turned
the radio on.
Music blared
in the backseat.
A few times
he caught me
looking at him.
Rain pelleted
the taxi.
A car honked.
Thunder exploding.
Lightning enflamed
the darkness.

Lesson in the Back of a Cab

My interpreter Lana
sat in the passenger seat.
Her husband, Mark,
and I were in the back.
The green-and-white cab
merged into traffic.
Motorbikes zigzagged
around us, beeping.

I told them I was in the mood
for bánh xèo, a Vietnamese crepe,
its flour yellowed from turmeric,
stuffed with bean sprouts,
onion, and ground meat.
The Khmer have the same dish
with a similar sounding name—
a name that refers to the sizzling
when flour and hot oil meet.
I wanted to taste the difference.

The bright city lights flashed
red, green, and yellow.
My mind turned to the night traffic
in Boston thirty-plus years ago
when our plane landed in America
after the war spilled into Cambodia.
Suddenly a motorbike cut
in front, almost hitting the cab, honked,
and sped away.

Crossing the Street in Hà Nội

Don't wait for when it's safe
to cross. There will never be a time.
Walk slowly, deliberately.
Mindful of your breath,
do not make sudden changes
in any directions.
You have to trust the motorcyclists.
Make eye contact with those nearing
you. Don't be brave, don't be scared,
don't be stupid. Remember, each
breath is sacred, a drop in the cosmic
ocean. If this is too much, look for
a native nearby, walk beside her,
cross when she crosses.
That's it, easy does it.
You're almost there.
Twenty more steps to go.
God help you.

Hà Nội Nights

Like crickets
the beep-beep of motorbikes
echoes throughout the night.
I am out of sync in the swarming
noise of trucks, cars, and bikes.
In this half-awake, eternal city
there is an unspoken pact,
an understanding in the marrow and air
even among the insane motorists,
a driver backing his truck against traffic,
a teenager racing through the lights,
where suddenly everything slows.
I then see her, gray pajamas,
face wrinkled, ashen hair
under conical hat, taking her time.
The drivers part for her
like the Red Sea, as she pedals
her rusty bicycle straight ahead,
without a care in this world, or the next.

Lady of Justice

1.

I asked Mark about the woman
in the conical hat, straight black
hair covering her shoulder and back.
"That's Our Lady of Justice," he said.
"She appears in different forms.
Sometimes, she rides her bicycle
with fruits and vegetables in her basket.
Other times, she carries a bamboo pole,
a scale of justice on her shoulders,
a ghost from the past, of wars,
duty, the old way of life.
She is eternal:
her hat bopping
in the busy Hà Nội street."

2.

A French tourist was having breakfast
with her husband on the second floor
of the May De Ville hotel when she put
down her knife and fork, pointed,
her painted red lips opened wide,
"Regarde, une ancienne femme!"
The husband grabbed his camera
from the table, walked up to the glass
wall and snapped photos of a woman
in gray pajamas and long sleeve shirt
carrying vegetables and fruits
from the countryside, her bamboo pole
bent by duty and sacrifice.
A swarm of motorbikes and cars
honked, slowed, and swirled,
an invisible sphere to protect her.

3.

She gets up at two in the morning,
washes her feet, hands, and face
with cool water from the well.
She bends down, legs folded,
blows into the crackling fire.
Dust and ash in the air
paint her face and fingers.
She stir-fries morning glories
with garlic and ginger.
The clay pot of rice simmers.
In her one-bedroom hut
her daughters wrap
their tiny arms around
their father. Near
the head of the bed is the altar
with candles and incense,
a picture of Hồ Chí Minh
next to a picture of her parents.
She's going to take a two-hour
bus ride into Hà Nội
to sell her fruits,
vegetables, and flowers,
hoping to sell enough
for the bus ride back
and a little extra
for books and pens
for her daughters.

Helicopter Mother on a Train to Huế

She wore elephant pants no Vietnamese
would be caught dead wearing.
Two conical hats. A huge water bottle.
Lonely Planet books on Southeast Asia
sprawled on the top bunk. When I saw her
I was happy. I missed the sound of English,
its taste on my tongue, the cheese on pizza
and steak bomb, Coca-Cola, TGIF's,
sit-down toilet, free napkins, being understood.
But this woman didn't want to hear any of it.
Her face glued to the guidebooks
as if she were searching for the Nam of her past,
of war and atrocities, in television and imagination,
maybe a brother or a first husband MIA
on Monkey Mountain in Da Nang.
Minutes later, a young man with blonde hair,
scruffy beard, and soft puppy eyes peeked in,
a tiny serpent tattooed on his right shoulder.
He saw me, smiled, "Cool. Another guy to party."
He turned to the American woman,
"Is it okay if I hang out with my Aussie buddies
in the other cabin?"

When the sun rose, the mother too rose,
covered her son with a blanket.
When the train stopped, she woke
her child up and asked, "Had fun
with your drinking buddies?"
The son rubbed sleep from his eyes
and murmured back: "Mah. Mah. Mah."

Beautiful Hội An

As if one day both sides agreed
to lay down their guns and shook
hands on a truce, admiring
the beauty of this coastal town,
its pagodas surrounded by dragons,
Chinese gods and goddesses,
its Japanese bridge guarded
by a pair of monkeys on one side
and a pair of dogs on the other.

At night the bright lanterns
float down the cool water,
fireworks light up the night sky.
Tourists swarm souvenir shops,
tea houses, bakeries, restaurants.
ATMs around one corner.
Vietnamese women, their faces
powdered, lips painted cherry,
wear their traditional áo dài in blue,
pink, and red. They walk up
to tourists: "Want mangoes?
Pineapples? Dragon fruits?"
I ask to take their picture.
They pose, smiling for the camera.
Their hands extended, open,
charge me one US dollar.

To the Blue-Eyed and Blonde-Haired Girl in a Hmong Village in Northern Việt Nam

Your father is not the American
who wants to be Rambo
returning to Việt Nam,
kissing the beautiful Vietnamese
woman before she is killed,
shooting his arrows
at every Vietnamese and Russian,
a perfect ending for Hollywood.

Your father is not the American
from Elizabethtown, New Jersey,
listening to 2 Live Crew's sampling
of the lines "Me Love You Long Time"
from Kubrick's *Full Metal Jacket*,
fantasizing about a prostitute
with long black hair
in a red miniskirt, shaking her tiny hips,
beckoning him to come
to her beautiful, ravaged country.

Your father is not the Dutch tourist
married with children.
A midlife crisis sends him
to Việt Nam.
In a trip up north to Sapa,
where tourists go to leave
behind the city's dense air
and heavy traffic,
he meets a young Hmong
from a local village
and leaves when his children
text him to come back home.

Those jeers and taunts
from the other children
are the terrible blooming
of envy and jealousy.
Difference provokes
fear, but also awe.
Your father is Chi You,
the tyrant, the God of War.
The weapon you wield
is the needle you use
to embroider cloths
with colorful patterns,
but whose symbols
are of your invention.
You provide new words
for breath, air,
three-headed elephant,
seed, snail, night sky,
chicken feet, ram's horn,
dragon's tail, sun,
and beautiful flower.

Squid Fishing in Halong Bay

A flashlight flickers
at the back of the deck
signaling the squid.
Around us darkness
and flickering lights
from other boats
as we drift into sleep.
The sun underneath us.

Mists rise from the green water.
Tiny vessels surround us,
and the stillness before war
is thick. The air is tense,
impossible to breathe.
Invaders from the north
in ships with cannons
and black death.
Then the miraculous happens.

From lapping waves a dragon rises,
its scales green, breath fiery,
and drops emeralds on the invading ships,
shatters them.
Those who survive sail
back to the land where a giant wall
winds like snakes
through great steppes of wild horses.
When the sea calms and the mists return,
the emeralds transform themselves
into mysterious limestone.

In a certain light
where the shade is one-fourth sea
green, these rocks move.

My Daughter Sleeps Tonight

My two-month old daughter sleeps
across the crib with giraffes,
baby elephants, lions, monkeys flying
above her. She's breathing heavily.
Snoring. Suddenly a cry comes
from her upturned lips, her right hand turns
to a fist like she's leading a revolution.

Her head with short dark, spiked hair
shakes from left to right.
Her little body twitches, then stills
for minutes until her clenched fists
flower into soft, tiny fingers, reaching out
through the flying animals to catch
stars that only she can see.

My wife and I stand around the crib,
our fingers clutching its bars: helpless.

Part II

Lies I Told about Father

I believed I had the power to revive you,
to sit you up in the family's pigsty,
drunk off your ass, smiling at nothingness,
with the late morning light shining your face.
With a son's quiet adoration, I chiseled you:
a gangster from the East, a Khmer Krom,
whose veins bled out Khmer characters (not Vietnamese),
who, guided by fate, found himself in the West
and married Mother for her virtue and beauty.

In my poems you drink because, well, real men
drink, curse, and sleep around
(the cursing and sleeping around, you didn't do,
because of your love and respect for Mother).
You see, I was an aspiring writer then,
renting a tiny studio on Ocean Boulevard,
in Long Beach, following in the drunken
bouts of Charles Bukowski, buying cheap wine,
imitating free verse,
waking up to the sour stench
of vomit and headache in the morning.
Of course, this life did not last long.
I couldn't hold liquor, let alone women.
I have always been a reader,
safe behind words, punctuations, and sentences,
between the pages, where I can conquer
an entire nation or seduce a woman with my long dash—.

Now, I am engaged to a kind, generous woman.
Mother would approve.
I am returning to you once again,
not for your approval, just to talk,
son to father, and then it dawns on me:
I am without you.

Logan Airport

Between the stillness
of early morning
and the rush
of rolling suitcases,
I was drawn to her.
Five-feet tall, rimmed
glasses, unassuming,
this tiny woman
sat next to me
in the lobby
of Japan Airlines.
Her voice soft,
accent like mine,
one who had lived
in the U.S. longer than
her native country.

She was returning
to Nakagawa
to see her parents
at the hospital.
She'd been in America
for forty years,
her children knew
little Japanese,
her grandchildren
couldn't distinguish
teriyaki and Chinese stir-fry.

I said I was going
to visit my father's village
for the first time.

She said to me,
"I wish I had instilled
Japanese culture in
my children and passed
it down to my grandchildren.
Now, I am flying home
alone to see my parents."

Searching for Father in Kampuchea Krom

1.

Two men sat
on a plush, beige sofa,
quiet and nervous,
in a hotel lobby
in downtown Saigon.
Their skin darkened
by work under the sun.
One wore sandals.
When he stood up
he wiped his hands
on his pants,
then reached out
to shake my hand.
I pressed my palms
close to my chest,
"Johm riab soor,"
then asked,
"Where's Lok-Yiey?"
"She's home waiting,"
he answered.
"She's old. She can't sit
in the car for very long."

At the hotel's parking lot
three women and another man
got out of a SUV, and smiled.
I waved, raised my hands,
said, "Johm riab soor."
I waved to a boy in the back.
I was given the passenger seat
because the A/C worked best.

The driver,
a light-skinned young man,
smoked cigarettes,
said very little.
From the back, one woman
offered oranges from her yard
while another kept grabbing
my arms, massaging my shoulders,
touching my cheeks, crying,
"I can't believe this is real!
I can't believe you are here!"

2.

After a four-hour ride
crossing bridges and highways,
passing farms and towns,
a rest stop midway for lunch
where my aunt kept putting
stewed pork on my plate,
the SUV stopped on a dirt road.
Kids ran around shirtless,
kicking up dust.
Men sat in front of their homes,
chatting, smoking, and staring.
I studied the thatched roof,
an old world slowly dislodging
in my mind's eye.
I was told that someone
was coming to pick me up
on a motorbike.
Where we were heading,
cars cannot pass through.

3.

My father's mother
wore a white shirt
and black sarong.
Head shaved,
teeth blackened
from betel nut.
Back bent,
just over four feet tall,
she came up to me,
touched my arms,
shoulders, and head.
No words spoken.
My aunts cried.
The young children
kept quiet.
The men sat
quietly apart.
An uncle broke
the silence,
"Go to the altar,
light six incense sticks:
three for your father,
three for your grandfather.
Tell them you are home."

4.

My grandmother spoke
with lead on her tongue,
as if each Khmer word was surrounded
by ten other Vietnamese words.
My uncles and aunts laughed
at my confusion. An aunt
explained, "She said Death
has visited her many times,
and each time she's told him
'No.' She must stay alive
to see her oldest child's son."
They sat around me.
"You are a special child.
You are able to come
to your father's village,
see your grandmother,
even though you live
many oceans away.
You are . . . ."
I didn't understand
the phrase she said.
She too slipped
into Vietnamese.

5.

They tucked me in like a child,
this nephew from America,
in his forties and recently a father.
My uncle went around the bed,
making sure the mosquito net
covered every corner, leaving
no chance for dengue fever.
His wife stood behind him,
checking to see if anything
was amiss. I said goodnight,
heard their bed creak,
then whispers and giggles.
Privacy was the mosquito net
and the darkness of the countryside.
My father once slept and ate here,
breathed this air, walked on this dirt.
The bed was hard, the pillows high,
my back ached. I tossed and turned,
wrestling with thoughts of him.

6.

The toilet was a hole
in the ground.
A brown clay jar stood
next to it. Sweat dripped.
A pitcher floated
in the spring water.
I caught myself
in the reflection.
Light skin, belly fat,
an American.
Young-looking,
even by Asian standards.
No running water.
Electricity powered by
one extension cord.
What am I doing here?
My knees trembled,
body soaked with fear.
I stumbled out.
My uncle looked up
from the kitchen table,
"Find everything okay?"

7.

After lunch, my uncles left
to tend their farms.
My aunts and I began talking,
and they told me this story.
"Your mother had two babies
before you, but they died
in infancy. So your parents
left Battambang, came here
to leave the loss behind."
I gripped the table.
"They lived here for three
months because of the war.
You were conceived here.
Don't you understand?
You are supposed to be back."

8.

Along a dirt path I walked
from my grandmother's home
to my oldest aunt's for lunch.
I heard singing and laughter
around a bend in the road.
Then came children riding
bicycles, waving and giggling.
The boys had on blue pants
and white shirts, the girls
their áo dài. They had returned
from their Vietnamese school.
On the weekend they would
learn the Khmer alphabet.
But for now, they were happy
to be together, riding home
for lunch, singing songs.
After they disappeared
I couldn't help but whistle
a tune I learned in a Thai
refugee camp, a song
about a singing parakeet.

9.

The best part about food
in the Mekong Delta
was not the fish caught
in the morning, kept
swimming in a clay jar,
then grabbed by an aunt,
cleaned, chopped, and thrown
into a red clay pot of boiling stew,
its flesh sweet and tender.
The best part was the fruits
picked in my uncle's backyard.
Coconuts, jackfruits,
mangoes, mangosteen,
and this particular fruit,
the shape and size of
a grapefruit, but sweet
and creamy on the inside.
They called it milk,
but I, an orphan, misheard
and called it mother's milk.

10.

I sat behind one uncle
and the others rode behind,
a caravan of motorbikes.
They wanted to show
me the Khmer temples
in their part of the world.
Every fifteen minutes
we stopped and marveled
at the mighty oaks that had
stood since Angkor times,
the artwork that told
the Buddha's life.
At the temple where my father
became a monk, I lit incense,
got down on my knees
and bowed three times,
my head touching the ground.
I walked by the pond,
under the cool shade
of the hundred-year-old trees.

My uncles then took me
to a noodle shack, whose owner
had cried forty years ago
when my father married my mother,
a woman from Cambodia.
She showed me a faded picture
of my father as a young monk.
He was light skinned, a mole
near the corner of his mouth,
a smile barely contained.
The lady with creases around
her eyes said in her accent,

"Your father was handsome."
I ate num banh chok.
It was as tasty
as the noodle I had
on the road to Angkor Wat.
When she cleared the table
the owner asked what I thought
about the noodles. I said,
"It's so good I feel like
I'm in the real Cambodia."

11.

"Your father,"
my aunt said,
"was generous,
his heart as big
as the sky."
She opened wide
her arms.
Her body leaned
to the weight of memories.
"He invited friends over,
bought them dinners.
He was a good big brother.
He used to come up
behind us, wrap
his arms around
our shoulders, tightly."
As she told the story
she wrapped her arms
around herself, head titled,
eyes closed, weeping.
My uncles sat
in their corners blinking,
staring at the chicken
pecking the dirt floor.

12.

My father walked up
to the Khmer Rouge
after they killed the children
and opened their stomachs
to eat the livers.
My father got down
on his knees,
clasped hands over head,
and begged them
for a sliver of a victim's liver
so that I would not starve.
While everyone was sleeping
my father snuck into the kitchen,
stole a branch of coconuts,
and buried them in the woods.
Each time I cried from hunger
he disappeared into the night,
dug up a coconut,
gave me the juice to drink
and with dirt-encrusted fingers
spooned out the flesh
for me, his only child.

1618

An assortment of fruits,
fresh produce, meat,
fish, eels, cow rib cages.
Chickens with legs tied
clucked at passersby.
Father went to this outdoor
market after passing his exams.
What lessons did he learn?
In a small tent my uncle
and I had grilled pork
with vermicelli, the most
delicious dish I had
in Việt Nam for two bucks.
I was slurping my noodles
when a man came over to us.
He spoke to my uncle first,
then looked at me and sat down.
"I know your father."
He said pointing to his chest,
"I was his right-hand man."
After a few sips of tea
he began. "You must know
our Khmer history.
From Saigon to the South
was part of the Khmer Empire
until our king took for wife
a beautiful Vietnamese woman.
He gave all this land to Việt Nam.
Saigon used to be called *Prey Nokor*
'til 1618, when it changed its name
to Saigon. Remember: 1618."
By the time he finished
the noodles were soggy and
the green chilies too spicy.

Dream of a Khmer Krom

He was a slim man,
hollow eyes and sharp
Adam's apple, smiled
when he spoke, as if
he found pleasure
in the stories he told.
But his stories were sad
like the shack he stayed
in at night to guard
the coconut tree farm.
The toilet, a wooden
platform perched
on the murky river
outside the shack.
The catfish swam out
of the mud, flopped about,
and splashed the water
when he used the toilet.

His companions were
the dim light bulb hanging
from a wooden beam
and a small color TV
tuned to a Khmer station
in Phnom Penh.
When he got bored
he put in a DVD
and watched
Khmer karaoke.
The moon lit up
the sky illuminating
the coconut field
and the rice farm.
His rusty pistol
hung on the wall.

Once, before having kids,
he visited Phnom Penh,
but as soon as he spoke
the Khmer people called
him "Vietnamese."
In southern Việt Nam,
where he was born,
he was a Khmer minority
receiving a bag of rice
each month for sending
his children to school.

He lit a cigarette,
took a deep breath,
as the Khmer women
danced on the TV,
shaking their small hips
to a song celebrating
the Cambodian New Year.
Young men and women
threw powder at each other.
The one time in the year
they came close to almost
touching one another.
Outside the frogs croaked,
and the crickets sang,
a constellation of night songs.
The rice field stood
quietly in the distance.

And So I Was Blessed

When I told my uncles and aunts
that I would be staying in Saigon
then traveling to Central Việt Nam
and finishing the last two months
of my semester in Hà Nội,
they looked at each other.
My uncle called the temple
where my father became a monk.
"The monk has to bless you,
clean you of bad karma."
He said after the phone call.
I said, "You have good and bad
people everywhere you go.
You have to pay attention.
Read people. Be smart.
Don't walk alone at night.
Don't act recklessly."
In response, they told stories.
Lifeless bodies found
in ditches along the road.
A lone traveler stopped,
beaten, and robbed.
A peasant ripped off
by city dwellers.
The victim was always
a villager who traveled
to the city for work.
I agreed to the cleansing
ceremony, not because
my uncles and aunts
were terrific storytellers.
Admittedly, I was nervous
about leading students
on trips all over Việt Nam
and not knowing the language.

What harm could it do me
to be washed in spring water
fragranced by incense,
perfume, and Champa flowers,
and blessed by a monk?

Part III

How to Prepare Yourself for a Semester Abroad in Việt Nam

Don't watch *Platoon* or *Apocalypse Now*.
That's about us Americans.
Don't rely heavily on those travel guides
like *The Lonely Planet* and *Insights Guides.*
Stay away from Food Network shows
like Bourdain's *No Reservations*
or Zimmerman's *Bizarre Foods.*
It's not a freak show.
If you live near a Vietnamese
American community, check out
its restaurant scene, eat the food
but not the politics. Be aware
there are many sides to a story.
And how does one put into words
waking up on a boat one morning
watching the sunrise at Hạlong Bay?
Or watching the chaos of Saigon
traffic and discovering its still point?
Or trekking up a mountain in Sapa
when suddenly you feel small
in the presence of the eternal?
Listen, try not to have expectations.
And don't read the poems in this book.

The Tall Blue-Eyed Kid from Long Island

Shares with the entire class,
"The study abroad manual
recommends the following:
Blend in with the environment.
Do not stand out.
But how do I do that
when I don't look like
everyone here?
At a restaurant where
they have these little
plastic tables and seats,
my knees tower
over the tabletop.
I'm like Godzilla.
When I walk the street
I can see the top
of everyone's head.
When I open my mouth
to ask directions
in the Vietnamese
we've been studying,
the woman turns
her head and blinks
her eyes."

And how do I,
his professor, advise him
when the only way
I can order food is by pointing
at the menu and smiling,
hoping our shared humanity
will be recognized,
or my Asian features read

as *Việt Kiều,*
maybe a long lost brother
or a son returned
from studying abroad
and forgiven for losing
his father tongue?

A Day in Saigon

Morning. I turned a corner
to my favorite phở shop
on Nguyễn Bình Khiêm.
I gave the proprietor
the number one sign,
walked to the back,
sat at a table near the door
where I could see steam
rising from metal cauldrons,
an old woman carving
thin beef slices. A young girl
placed a dish of wilted
bean sprouts and green chilies,
an extra dish of my favorite mint:
one that reminded me
of a dish my aunts made
in the Mekong Delta.
With chopsticks I shoveled
the noodles into my mouth,
shaking off a sleepless night
of missing wife and child.

Noon. At a stall next to my apartment
I pointed to the grilled meat and fish,
found a seat near the local students.
A woman stopped by my table,
placed a dish of wilted cabbage
over steamed rice, a bowl of soup,
a plate of fish and meat covered
with sweet and tangy sauce.
Like my young cousins in America
the students talked, laughed,
and checked their phones.
There was no memory of war
as they slurped up the tasty Phở
and checked their Facebook status.

Evening. The Saigon heat
still burned, shirt stuck
to chest with sweat.
At a stall on a crowed street
a woman in black pants turned
a lever, squeezing the sugarcane,
juice flowing out.
She scooped it into a plastic cup
with crushed ice.
I gave her 20,000 dong
and refused the change.
On a bench I took a sip
from the cup, concentrated
on the cane's sweetness,
as I tried to rid myself
of a film I showed students
that afternoon.
An entire village destroyed.
Corpses of women and children
tossed in ditches, left
on a dirt road to the rice fields.
One woman, her legs splayed,
and a child below her,
his head missing,
as if he were crawling
back into the womb.

It Hit Me

In my air-conditioned apartment
in District 1 of Hồ Chí Minh City
I turned on my Macbook Air,
studied photos of my daughter.
One with her in a yellow rocker,
hair disheveled,
arms reaching up,
smiling,
brows furrowed
to form questions,
bright eyes
staring right
at me.

A Reasonable Explanation

My students and I were on a boat
floating down the Mekong.
Armed with cameras, water bottles
and curiosity, we took pictures
of everything around us.
Houses on stilts. Fishing boats
congregated to form a floating market,
farmers selling squashes, tapiocas, fish.
A dingy with a motor came up
to our boat. Students snapped photos.
A woman smiled, "Cà phê sữa đá?
Cà phê nóng?"
Seeing the hot brown coffee
splashing in a plastic water bottle,
my students grew quiet.
Another boat pulled up next to ours
selling "nước ngọt," sodas.
Again, we shook our heads.
The two boats sped away.
Water sprayed our sun-dried faces.
Further down the river we saw
fishermen taking a break.
They jumped and dove off
a dilapidated plank.
A student took her camera out
and began snapping.
One of the men reached down
underneath his shorts
and began washing himself.
We laughed. The student turned
and asked, "What's so funny?
It's good to have proper hygiene."

Daughter

I must ask for your forgiveness
for any mistakes I might make.
I only want what is best for you.
Remember, joy is not wealth,
which enslaves the psyche
and destroys the spirit.
Joy is the love you share
with family and friends and the respect
you show towards all that is life.
Choose whatever path speaks to you.
Make it moral and righteous.
When lost, return to books,
music, and arts.
They will help you find your way.
Strength is not found in might.
It is your mother waking up at 4 a.m.
to check if you are breathing.
It is your father leaving home
searching for his own father
in the cries and laughter
of his aunts and in the furtive
glances of his uncles.
And hope resides
in lonely rice fields
when your father, lost,
thinks of your mother
and you, and smiles.

People Watching

Evening. After a monsoon-like rain
that flipped umbrellas inside out
and bent thousand-years old trees
leaving debris scattered all over the streets,
I sat on a plastic seat on the sidewalk
sipping sugarcane juice. I didn't want
to go to my apartment. No one was there.
A young man sat not far from me,
his satchel slung over his shoulders.
Smartphone out, he pressed the screen,
his face lit up. Another man pulled over
his motorbike and ordered sugarcane juice.
He sat staring at the quiet traffic.
What thoughts went through his head?
A country girl he left in the countryside
to work in this lonely city?
Then a father and daughter walked by.
A puddle lay in their path.
The father lifted his daughter gently
with both hands. Her legs kicked,
as if she were air walking.

On a Motorbike in Saigon

An old friend from graduate school
came to pick me up on his motorbike.
He tossed a helmet at me, revved
up the engine, and said, "Let's go!"
I hopped on, both hands gripping
the seat, as we swerved with traffic.
He was trying to make small talk,
then asked where I'd like to eat.
"I don't care," I yelled back,
screaming against the noise
of motorbikes, cars, and buses,
against the rain and lightning,
against the road's slickness.
I answered, "The closer, the better."
He thought a bit, then said,
"Think of this as a video game.
You turn left. You dodge right.
It's all fun." I said, "Except
my life is on the line. And
I need to get back home and
see my wife and daughter."

We stopped at an intersection.
No one was making eye contact.
Engines hummed to the song
the rain made, then everyone
began revving, like some mating
ritual. The bikes inched forward
before the lights even changed.
"This is madness!" I said.
My friend laughed,
then began quizzing me
on the Vietnamese
I had learned that day.
Before I could answer

he cut in front of a taxi
and sped away from impact.
I heard someone honk,
watched a taxi fly by us.
A prayer overcame me:
"Oh fuck, oh fuck, fuck me."

On Our Way to a Famous Cave
in Central Việt Nam

The cave was in a mountain,
and inside were stalagmites rising
from the cold clear water
and stalactites hanging from the roof,
a crystal palace of blue
and purple radiating.
With a name like Paradise Cave,
who wouldn't want to see it?
So we drove out from Chu Lai.
The students were restless, but tired.
Some stared at the endless green.
A few worked on their laptops.
Most slept. An hour later,
one student asked about stopping
for a bathroom break.
The guide said we would stop
at the center of town.
Twenty minutes later another
student tapped my shoulder.
The guide gave the same answer.
I looked out the window. Nothing
resembling a town was in sight.
I turned around. My students
were fidgety, eyes blinking
at me. I thought of my daughter,
how I held her in my arms,
kissed her forehead before
I left for Việt Nam.
I stood up and asked,
"How many of you need to use
the restroom?"
Half had their hands up.
"If I have the bus stop here,
how many of you are willing

to go into the woods?"
"You mean pee out there?"
I nodded.
A few raised their hands.
I told the guide to tell the driver
to find the safest place to stop.
Once the driver turned off
the engine and opened the door,
a few kids ran out.
More followed until the bus
was empty.
American students with shorts
and t-shirts, water bottles,
made tracks for the woods.
One ran out laughing
and said she was almost bitten
by ants while peeing.
Others joined in the laughter.
I told the guide to bring
out the packed lunch.
Together, professor and students,
guide and bus driver,
devoured rice and noodles,
gulped down warm bottled water
in the middle of nowhere.

After a Letter from Cambodia Delivering News of Father's Death

At seventeen, you were already weary.
The world sat heavy on your shoulders.
You were a tiny red bird,
wings broken and beaks cracked.
There were no songs to sing.
You thought about using a gun
but that would leave a mess
for your poor grandmother
to clean up.
The rope was cheap
but suffocating.
Pills were the way to go,
painless and clean.
Maybe it was fate,
or the body's will was stronger
than your own.
Maybe the cosmos was not ready
to reabsorb your energy.
You escaped that night
vomiting all the pills you took,
head between knees, weeping.

Years later
you met your wife,
had a child,
a daughter whose smiles
lit up the stars,
a daughter who taught
you the joyful songs
you were meant
to sing.

Hotel in the Clouds

The hotel sat on top of a mountain.
Clouds and mist surrounded us.
The sun was setting when we arrived.
The air was light and translucent.
When I opened the door to my room,
turned on the light, insects were flying,
some on my pillows and bed sheets.
I closed the windows, walked
the stairs, and tried to explain
to the receptionist about the insects.
I saw the guide and called him.
Nothing they could do, I was told.
I had to open the windows,
turn off the light, and hope
the insects would fly out
towards the balcony light.
I walked down the steps,
saw a few students milling
in front of a room and laughing.
One walked out of the room,
"Professor, there's poop
on my bed." I thought to myself,
God, I hope it's animal poop,
not some sick prankster shitting
on the bed as some twisted joke.
I told him, "Listen, I'm not going
in there. I'll take your word. Go
to the lobby and tell the guide."

In my room I turned off
the light, opened the windows,
turned on the balcony light
when I heard voices in the hallway.
I opened the door, peeked
my head out, and noticed students

in front of another door.
I saw Lana, my Vietnamese
translator, and asked.
"What's going on?"
"They're locked inside.
The door handle doesn't work."
I asked the two students
stuck inside their room,
"Are you guys okay?"
"We're fine, professor."
Soon, the hotel manager
arrived, asked me to tell
the students to turn the metal
ring around the doorknob.
They tried, but to no avail.
When the locksmith arrived
he unscrewed the washer,
pushed the screwdriver
into the door hole,
and the knob fell out.
Everyone cheered.
The door opened
to the students
smiling sheepishly.
I said, "I hope you weren't
too worried about food.
We could have brought dinner
through the bars on the balcony.
Speaking of food, the hotel
has set up dinner in the lobby.
Let's go. I'm starving."

After supper we went
to our separate rooms.
I closed the door, unpacked,

and charged my phone.
I washed my face, flossed,
and brushed my teeth
when screams came, again,
from the hallway.
This time the noise came
from three female students.
They were laughing
and pointing to a corner
of their room.

A huge spider
with thin long legs
sat quietly still
while students took
turns walking up
to it and taking pictures
with their smartphones.
"Dude, we gotta put
this on Facebook
and Instagram."
"This is so crazy,"
another student laughed.
"This is Việt Nam,"
someone chimed in.
Minutes later a man
with a cook's apron
showed up, holding
a pair of chopsticks.
He stopped at the wall,
looked up, and grabbed
the spider with his chopsticks
while the students burst
out laughing and screaming.
The cook left with

the spider's legs kicking
the chopsticks
while the students' screeching
deafened my ears.

That evening, my body tensed.
I did what I hadn't done in a long time:
I got down on my knees and prayed,
asking the mountain spirits
for forgiveness, protection,
and a safe journey for all of us.
I closed my eyes and heard wings
flapping over my head:
a butterfly must have flown
through the window while I prayed.
I turned off the lights,
dreamed about my daughter
laughing as I tickled her chin
and kissed her head.

After a Dream

I wake up.
Alone in an apartment
in Hà Nội.
The air is humid, heavy.
Constant honking
of motorbikes.
A man runs across
the street for
his cà phê đá.
I wash my face
in the sink.
Outside the rain falls,
heavy and fast,
thudding against sidewalks,
umbrellas, walls, windows,
throbbing inside my head.
I am a small boat
bereft at sea,
a child orphaned
once again.

At the Edge of Khau Phạ Pass

"Hey Professor," they giggled.
I glanced up: a student was standing
on the edge of a cliff,
green abyss below,
clouds on his shoulders,
one leg lifting, hands stretched out,
like Christ the trickster,
his roommate snapping photos
to be shared later on Facebook.
All it took was an unruly pebble,
a gush of cruel wind,
or the hand of an indifferent God.
My mind flashed
a letter to the parents:
Dear Mr. and Mrs. So & So,
I regret to inform you
that your son . . . .
My knees wobbled.
I squinted my eyes,
gritted my teeth,
the cold mountain wind
brushed my hot cheeks.
I walked slowly
towards the student,
said as calmly as I could,
"You're too close to the edge.
Stand nearer the railing, please."

Không Biết Tiếng Việt

Hà Nội hums with the sounds
of motorbikes running and people chatting.
Sidewalks are littered with plastic tables
and chairs, men sipping coffee,
leisurely watching a four-way intersection.
Women selling and buying,
some call to me to sit at their tables
for fried rice, soup, and pickled vegetables.
With a bag of vegetables, oil, and soy sauce
from a local grocery store, I smile
and amble around shops and sidewalk cafes,
stepping onto the street
with cars flying inches from me.
I stop at a light and wait for it to change
when a motorbike stops in front of me.
In white surgical mask, long shiny black hair,
eyelashes curved upward, a woman begins
asking me questions in Vietnamese.
Her right arm raised and finger pointing
to what is ahead of her.
I smile politely, "không biết tiếng Việt."
Then I say it in English to convince myself
the truth of such statement, "I don't know
Vietnamese." Eyes down, I shake my head
as the light changes. The woman rides away.
Her black hair dances in the northern wind.

Visiting a Hmong Village in Northern Việt Nam

1.

There were twenty of us, including
a guide from the local Hmong village.
I carried a cellphone, bottled water,
and a point-and-shoot camera.
A first-aid kit in my backpack.
We trekked up the mountain.
The incline made my feet heavy,
the sun high and bright on my head.
My shirt soaked my chest and back.
And below us was open space,
terraced rice fields of bright green.
I was transported into another world:
thatched-roof huts, houses on stilts,
barefoot children carrying branches
looking for crabs and fish
hidden in the mud.
Like an invading army
we took out our cameras
aimed and shot, knowing
we would never be able
to capture such beauty:
A boy using a stick to roll
a car tire along a dirt road.

2.

Two students who had
became close friends
stopped next to a hut
that hung over a cliff,
below a green sea
of rice fields scattered

on the mountainsides.
They took out their cameras,
got on their knees
as if to pray, then snapped
photos of this home.
I shook my head.
When I reached the hut
I saw an elderly woman
sewing bright red cloth,
a naked child sitting
beside her. I too took
out my camera and began
snapping pictures.

3.

We stopped in the town square—
the main road cut through
with a few shanty stores on each side.
A student bought what looked
like a hybrid of an apple and a pear.
He was practicing his Vietnamese
with the locals, smiling as he bit
into the fruit. His friend,
whose father was black
and mother Canadian,
stood next to him, quiet
and reserved, respectful.
The local people began
to gather around him.
They spoke in their dialect,
pointing at his hair.
One man walked up
to my student, pointed

at his head, then touched his.
"They want to touch
your head," his roommate said.
My student lowered his head.
The man reached out,
pet his curly hair, then pulled
away, laughing. The crowd hollered.
Then another man came over,
touched my student's hair,
and quickly pulled away.
More laughter.
We took out our cameras,
snapped photos, then stopped,
switched things up a bit
by having our pictures
taken with the local people.
I stood next to a young man,
six inches shorter than me,
his body tight and lean,
smiling his toothless smile,
staring curiously straight
into the camera.

4.

On the path winding
down the mountainside,
little children and their siblings
came out to watch me limp along,
my body heavy with sweat.
I waved, they waved back.
They giggled, their round faces
bright, eyes shyly cast away.
A grandmother walked over,

put down her heavy basket,
took out colorful scarfs, bags,
and headgears. I shook my head,
smiled, and resumed walking:
knowing that this place
would change in a few years
with more tourists,
when the local people
learned that their cultures,
the clothes on their backs,
could be exchanged for money.

The Other Is Me

Passing through a village
in Sapa, a student points
to a rice field on our left.
Five little kids with a bucket
and sticks poke at the wet dirt.
My mind turns to a girl
I knew thirty-five years ago.

We were hungry, our parents'
backs bending in the fields.
The girl, a few years older,
led the way as I followed
with a bucket crawling
with tiny black crabs.
The air smelled of dung,
dirt, and rotten leaves,
our bare feet squished
the warm muddy earth.

My friend poked each
hole with a stick.
A smooth entrance meant
an eel had slithered in the cavern.
A jagged one meant a crab
hiding in its damp abode
to keep cool from the sun.

My make-believe wife crouched
in front of a smooth entrance
poking a branch at it when
a forked tongue hissed,
and a black slimy body
slithered out sideway,
fast, erratic, unpredictable.

I yelled, "Get away."
She jumped back and fell.
The snake slithered towards her,
then past her.
Quickly as it appeared
it disappeared underneath rustling leaves.

No Longer the Tourist

Who snaps photos
of government buildings,
monuments, Hoàn Kiếm lake,
the Opera House, the Hỏa Lò prison
where John McCain was kept
for five-and-a-half years.
Now I cringe at a caravan of cyclos
pedaled by tired, ashen-haired
Vietnamese men biking a Western
family around the lake.
The father cranes his neck
to take a selfie with his wife.

The Temple of Literature no longer
moves me the way it once did.
Once the hair on my arms and neck swayed
in humility and admiration.
Now I see it for what it is: a tourist trap.
People all over the world flock
to Việt Nam's first national university
to take photos of the Great Confucius
and rub the smooth, polished statues
of the turtle and crane,
symbols of longevity and power.
At the temple's exit gate,
you are greeted with middle-aged women
trying to sell you T-shirts that read
"Good Morning Vietnam,"
"Phở Metal Jacket,"
and "Make Phở, Not War."

Thanksgiving in Hà Nội

The doorbell started ringing
around 7. The students placed
their sneakers by the door,
not wanting to invite
evil spirits to my apartment.
Then dinner arrived:
sandwiches and pumpkin
pies from the tourist district
on the other side of the lake.
Someone was missing
a turkey sandwich.
In the spirit of friendship
each donated a small bit
of his or her sandwich.
Soon, there was enough
food for everyone.
Someone shouted,
"This is what Thanksgiving
is all about!"
And everyone laughed.

The winning movie
was "Lost in Translation."
All of us crammed
in my living room.
Some on the couch
and love seats.
Most on the floor
with food on their laps.
I sat on a chair
close to the TV.
We were all glued
to the screen.
We laughed uncomfortably
when Murray's character

was confused, got frustrated,
did not understand
what he was supposed
to do or say shooting
a Suntory's commercial
or when the treadmill
kept spinning out on him.
Like us, all he could do
was hold on tight.

We grew quiet
when Murray's character
wandered in crowded Tokyo streets
or stuck with Johansson's
in an elevator where they were
the only foreigners in a sea of Asians.
My thoughts turned to my students.
They had been good,
responsible, adventurous
but not reckless,
just curious and smart,
in search of the other
only to find it in themselves.
When someone fell sick
or behind, they made sure
to let me know immediately.
They held fireside chats to talk
about what they went through.
Then I thought about my wife
and our six-month old daughter.
On Skype I'd been beaming
with pride to see my daughter
holding a spoon to her mouth,

and was filled with envy
from seeing my baby girl sleep
on my wife's shoulder.

In this apartment in Hà Nội,
far from wife and daughter,
Domino pizzas, Italian subs,
fat, juicy, artery-choking bacon
and creamy cheeseburgers,
Chinese food made for non-Chinese tongues,
far from that autumn smell when fallen
leaves mixed with rain and cold air,
my students were trying to pick up
on what Murray's character whispered
to Johansson's ear
when the Jesus and Mary Chain's
"Just Like Honey" came on,
the credits rolled,
and I felt pride and joy,
and luck, lots of luck.

Flying from Hong Kong to Los Angeles

From fear, silver pearls of sweat
glistening my forehead.
I uttered the names of my mother,
father, grandfather, then of
the grandmother whom I lost
earlier in the year.

The last three weeks
in Việt Nam
I tossed and turned,
got up for a glass of water,
turned on my laptop
and studied the photos
of my daughter.
Her eyes wide,
her smiles wider.
I repeated her name
in the darkness
until sleep took over.

When the plane lifted off
and below was the blueness
of the Pacific,
thoughts that I'd never see
my daughter overwhelmed me.

Whatever happens
I can't have my daughter
be fatherless.
She will not share
my fate,
a stranger among peers,
one who envies friends
for having parents,
whose sadness

sits heavy and stirs
when she sees
a little girl
arms like an airplane
flying high
on her father's shoulders.

A married couple
sat to my left.
Heads tilted together.
Their eyes closed.
Hands clutching.

Waiting in LAX for a Flight to Boston

The guy behind the counter
looked as if I were bothering him
when I placed my order.
I felt like apologizing afterward.
At Le Club Café in Hà Nội
I had been greeted by the young waitresses
who smiled and nodded.
And they didn't expect tips.

The burrito and a small cup of fountain
pink lemonade cost a little over ten dollars
while a pork bánh mì and cà phê sur đá
at the Coffee House in Saigon
were about two U.S. dollars.

The carne asada burrito
was too big for my Asian stomach.
I left a third of it for dinner.

Boarding an American Airlines plane
I walked through business class
where each passenger had his own
spaceship, sitting or reclining
in his private throne, watching TV,
reading a book, or using his smart phone.
His arm, the size of my body.
His stomach seemed ready
to burst through his shirt
a dozen green baby aliens.

I found my seat next to a guy
with a New England Patriot jacket
and beer belly. His face glowed
from the laptop screen.
He placed his left arm
on the elbow rest between us.

Trời ơi, Trời ơi

"Em ơi," I called
to the barista in Vietnamese.
When he returned with iced
coffee, I said, "cảm ơn, em."

After a sip I spat the coffee
back into its chilled tall glass.

When the bill arrived
I did a double take
and questioned
the ethics of tipping.

The streets were uneven.
The noise came through
in shards of broken glass.
The air felt strange, cold.

With the light still green
I crossed the street.
A car swerved, someone yelled,
"Jesus, get out of the road!"
And I mumbled a prayer:
"trời ơi, trời ơi."

For a minute I was back
in Saigon: two children
riding a bicycle in a crowded
alley. The boy pedaled,
the girl sat on the rack
behind the seat, her legs
hanging to one side.
A car honked.
The girl held the boy,
head pressed against his back.

The boy rose up, pumped his bike,
and hollered in sweet delight,
"trời ơi, trời ơi."

Song for Stella

My wife is in her third trimester.
This is when every position is
uncomfortable: sitting, standing,
lying sideways or on her back.
She finds herself out of breath
walking up a few steps of stairs.
At night I pick up my guitar,
sit in front of the computer,
turn to webpages with lyrics and chords.
I strum, my wife sings to our unborn daughter.
But I'm not a good keeper of time.
I switch chords too soon, or too
late, and my wife already annoyed
with the discomfort of sitting, glares.
She likes order, structure, constancy.
She endures my inconsistency.
Closing her eyes, she focuses only
on our daughter who at first breath
will recognize our sounds.

Postscript

Stranger

My daughter cried and cried
the first few hours she saw me.
She cried until she exhausted
herself to sleep. When she woke
up, I was still in her room.
Who was this stranger who looked
like her sitting on her bed?
She burrowed her face on her mother's
breasts and cried muffled cries.
The next morning I took out
my guitar, strummed the C and A
minor chords, then she stopped crying,
watched my playing, and smiled.

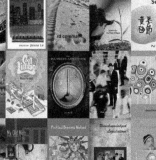

CPSIA information can be obtained
at www.ICGtesting.com
Printed in the USA
FSHW01n0506010918
51874FS